THE BiG book of ENERGiZERS

Jenny Mosley and Zara Niwano

Positive Press

Published in 2009 by:
Positive Press Ltd
28A Gloucester Road
Trowbridge
Wiltshire BA14 0AA

Telephone: 01225 719204
Fax: 01225 712187
E-mail: positivepress@jennymosley.co.uk
Website: www.circle-time.co.uk

Text © Jenny Mosley and Zara Niwano
Re-printed 2010
ISBN 1-904866-27-5

Illustrator: Mark Cripps

Printed in the U.K. Heron Press, www.heronpress.co.uk

Contents:

What are Energizers?

Most of us will be familiar with that awful sinking feeling when we realise that our children are drifting away and losing their zest for learning. We all know of occasions when everyone seems to have wandered off-task and we need to find ways to rein them in and get them focused again. The Big Book of Energizers is a toolbox crammed full of quick activities to do just that in a fun and non-confrontational way.

How can Energizers help?

Learning is about concentrating; retaining information and using it in ever more complex ways. As educators, we ask children to sit at a desk and concentrate for a long time. Sometimes this means that they lose contact with their need to release physical energy and lessons descend into scenes of fidgeting, irritability, children disturbing their neighbours or drifting off into daydreams that have nothing to do with the task at hand. When you notice that concentration and motivation are flagging, you need to stop and do something quick that wakes everyone up and pulls them back to task. You can do this by offering a complete change of scene that revitalizes their brains without utilizing the thoughtful task orientated part of the brain that is needed for your lesson. In other words, you need to give everyone a break, a tiny bit of play-time, a burst of physical joyfulness that brightens everyone up.

It is worth noting that the Calmers book works in a similar way by orchestrating a mental change of direction. With Energizers, this change of direction is away from listlessness and into focused alertness; whereas, with Calmers, children are being redirected away from anxiety or over-excitement and towards calm alertness. In other words, the same result is achieved but the starting points are different. This is why, sometimes, Energizers and Calmers can appear similar.

When can you use Energizers?

Anytime you think it might help! Energizers could be used once, twice or three times a day: any time that you want to enliven, awaken and re-focus your class after they have become fidgety or are feeling sluggish. However, when children come in from play or have become wound-up, we recommend that you use a Calmer from *The Big Book of Calmers*.

Who can use Energizers?

Anyone who facilitates a group of learners can use Energizers. We have designed this book for use in primary and secondary schools. However, most of the activities can be adapted for use in an early years setting or with children with special educational needs or for older children. Very young children naturally have a shorter attention span than older children and are frequently more in need of Energizers to help them stay focused.

Weary staff and enthusiastic parents can benefit from Energizers too!

What type of activities do we include in our Energizers?

There are few limits to what you could use, but generally, we like to include physical activity, popular themes and the use of the senses. These can include:

- clapping games
- singing games
- follow-my-leader games
- miming to a story or a theme
- using kinaesthetic learning opportunities
- games or activities involving simple touch
- using activities to consolidate classroom or healthy living routines
- using drumming, rhythm and rhyme
- challenges for children who need to stretch their minds as well as their muscles.

Each chapter of Energizers is grouped in a particular order. You will find them by the following symbols:

 1. **Thumbs up** = **activity can be played quickly and easily**

 2. **Index finger on the chin** = **game will take a bit of organising by the teacher**

 3. **Pointing outside** = **game will need a large space**

Before you get started

Here are some useful points to think about before you start using Energizers:

- If you are asking children to run on the spot or twirl their arms round, do they have room to do so without knocking into each other?
- Do you know how to stop children from working or fidgeting and ask them to start your Energizer? It is best to work out a little routine.
- Do any of your pupils have special requirements that could make any of the activities difficult, embarrassing or awkward for them?
- For your first few times using Energizers, have you planned them really well, so that you don't have to focus upon what to do and when, but can focus upon actually working with the children and enjoying the activity?
- Have you got a list of Energizers to hand that you can use whenever you need them, with different themes to suit the mood of the class?
- Have you thought how to make the Energizers more enjoyable for the class? For example, by joining in yourself, by putting on music or incorporating jokes and smiles?
- Will you use plenty of praise to compliment those who co-operate with each Energizer activity, listen well to you and do the activities well?
- Can you explain how to do the Energizers so that each child understands your expectations? Children will become frustrated if they do not understand what is expected.
- Will you be able to show the children your enthusiasm and happiness at having an activity break from the lesson? Let the children know it's a treat and a break and that you think it is fun - your enthusiasm is infectious!
- It is vital to involve everyone and experience tells us that giving some children the right to opt out and carry on working is likely to lead to other children doing this who may only pretend to be working while secretly hoping to cause a distraction. Try to be very quick when you introduce the activity so that rebellious children don't have time to think of reasons not to join in.
- Encourage the children to drink plenty of water – a dehydrated brain does not work effectively.
- For activities that are challenging, it might be appropriate for a teaching assistant or other pupil to work in a pair with any pupil who has a learning disability, or has a limited understanding of English, to support their contribution.
- Brave schools know that staff need Energizers too! If your colleagues are coming into meetings looking stressed and drained, why not try out a few Energizers with them and see if they catch on.
- Have you thought what routine or signal you could use to stop the Energizer session and ask children to re-focus upon their books, the board or your lesson? You need a quick and effective re-focusing routine to get back to the lesson – see page 4 for the 'Hand Up' routine.

All teachers need to train children to respond quickly and efficiently when the situation requires an instant response. We recommend that you use the following excellent technique whenever you do a Energizer.

The Hand Up Approach to Silence

Hold your arm up very straight and high.
Say NOTHING.

Stand very still and wait.

Children must respond by putting their hand up and touching the shoulders of others who are talking – who then put their hands up.

Bring your hand down.

Say, *'Thank you'*.

(Sometimes you can hold your hand up closed with a smiley-face sticker hidden inside it and give this to the first child to respond, and watch the ripple of attention!)

Physical Energizers

The activities in this section recharge the children's energy through stretching, moving and breathing exercises.

Our brains are part of our physical being and need to be constantly supplied with glucose, oxygen and other chemicals that feed brain cells and improve their efficiency. The brain makes use neurotransmitters, like dopamine, so that we can think clearly and remain alert and focused. Many activities in this section are designed to ensure that the brain gets the energy it needs by increasing the heart rate and improving circulation.

Other activities are gentler, and involve mind-body exercises in which the whole body works as one. This settles the child, lowers stress and nourishes the brain in a quiet and thoughtful way, which also renews and releases new energy.

Giving your class a short break from schoolwork and allowing them time to stretch and move their muscles will pay dividends in increasing ability to concentrate and remember what they are learning.

1. Oooh-Aaah opposite game

This energizer helps children stretch out, improves circulation and relaxes them through laughter.

What you need: nothing

What to do:

Teach children the following activity, explaining the key first.

Key

Aaah – stretch up to the ceiling and shout, 'Aaah', with joy.
Oooh – bend knees and put hands towards the floor. Say, 'Oooh', as if you've noticed something amazing.

Call out *'Oooh'* or *'Aaah'* in any order you choose. You can speed up or slow down and vary your tone of voice. The children then do the opposite to you. If you stretch and shout, *'Aaah'* – they crouch. If you crouch and shout, *'Oooh'* – they stretch and say, 'Aaah'.

Tip: Ask a child to come and be the caller at the front. See if the children can come up with a third and fourth call and action. For instance:

'Me' – point at self
'You' – point at another person.

2. Rumbling tums

This energizer requires children to perform two different actions at the same time, improving acuity and concentration.

What you need: nothing

What to do:

Ask children to tap their heads lightly with one hand, whilst gently rubbing their tummies round and round with the other hand.

When children have the hang of this, ask them to do the activity with the opposite hands, which will usually make it more difficult.

Ask one of the children to be the demonstrator at the front and see if they can think of another action to do whilst either rubbing their tummy or patting their head.

3. Freeze/thaw

This energizer involves quick changes of activity and motivates children to be alert and ready to respond quickly.

What you need: nothing

What to do:

Give the children a sequence of actions to do, like:

- running on the spot

- clapping their hands

- touching their toes

- reaching for the stars.

Call out an activity that children must start.
When you call, *'Freeze'*, the children stop what they are doing, stand very still and, instead, draw something in the air with their hand. They can draw any shape you choose – square, heart, snowflake, house, etc.

After a few seconds, call out, *'thaw'.*

Now they must resume the sequence of action until you call, *'freeze'*, again.

4. Touch game

This energizer gives children an excellent opportunity for revitalizing movement without leaving their seats.

What you need: nothing

What to do:

Tell the children to touch something with their thumb, little finger, elbow, knee, etc. For example, *'Touch the floor with your elbow'*; *'Touch your teeth with your little finger'*; *'Touch your nose with your thumb'.*

Tip: Think of some more difficult commands or ask them to do this with their eyes shut to encourage good listening.

5. Ready for action

This energizer requires that children must watch your signals, which tell them what to do, raising alertness through attentive watching.

What you need: space to sit on the floor

What to do:

Ask the children to sit on the floor.

Show the children a selection of actions that correspond with visual cues. For instance:

- when you clap your hands, everyone stands up and waves their arms

- when you touch your head, everyone hops up and down

- when you tap your knees, everyone sits down.

6. Tap down

This energizer uses gentle tapping actions to re-energize children's bodies and minds.

What you need: space for each child to stand in

What to do:

Ask the children to stand up with a little space around them.

Show them how to cup their hands loosely so that their fingers point down like a bird's feet.

Tell them that they must use their cupped fingers very gently.

Start with their heads – with very loosely cupped hands, gently tapping with light fingertips over their heads then down the backs of their necks.

They can then tap across the tops of their shoulders and down each arm with the other hand.

Then they tap gently down their fronts, their backs, the fronts and sides of their legs, ending at their feet.

When children have tapped all over the tops of their feet, tell them to flop like rag dolls just for a moment, before gently uncurling and coming back up to a standing position.

Finish with a big stretch upwards.

7. Wriggles

This energizer requires children to concentrate on doing two things at once, which stimulates their brain and improves their circulation.

What you need: nothing

What to do:

Ask the children to jog gently on the spot. While they are doing this, ask them to:

- wriggle their fingers

- wriggle their fingers and shake their hands

- wriggle their fingers, shake their hands and shrug their shoulders

- wriggle their fingers, shake their hands, shrug their shoulders and move their heads from side to side.

8. Countdown

This energizer calls for children to observe body language carefully and respond promptly, which invigorates their bodies and minds.

What you need: nothing

What to do:

This activity is best done in a circle or sitting in a way that enables them to look round and see each other.

To begin with, children are all sitting but, one at a time, each child stands up. As they stand, they call out their number. Like this: first child says *'one'*; second child says *'two'*; and so on. This continues until everyone is standing.

Then they count backwards, one number at a time, until they are all sitting down again. This means that they must remember their number from the first stage of the activity.

When the countdown gets to one, all the children jump, raise their arms and shout, *'LIFT OFF!'*

9. Heart beats

This energizer teaches children about the benefits of jogging while, at the same time, learning about healthy hearts.

What you need: nothing (optional: a basic picture of a heart)

What to do:

Start by asking children where their heart is, how big it is and what it does.

> *(The heart is on the left-hand side of the rib cage, about the size of an orange. It pumps blood all around the body to take nutrients and oxygen to the whole body and to remove wastes like carbon dioxide.)*

Tell the children that some of the things we do are said to be good for the heart, like active playing, healthy sport, healthy food, and that some things are said to be bad for the heart, like smoking, sitting around too much and eating junk food.

Ask the children to jog on the spot for ten counts if you shout out something which is good for the heart, but if you shout out something potentially bad for the heart, they flop down in their chairs.

- playing football
- eating too many sugary things
- watching hours of TV
- going for a walk
- eating salads
- playing for too long on the computer
- smoking cigarettes
- drinking fruit juice.

Ask the children to come up with more ideas – then they can run the game!

10. Eraser juggling

This energizer helps children to strengthen their dominant hand while the concentration it requires invigorates their brains.

What you need: a small, light ball for each child, or a pencil rubber

What to do:

Ask children to throw and catch the ball just with their writing hand. Their other hand could be behind their back or used to catch the ball if it goes astray. As they become more confident, bring in more elements of ball control. You can ask them to clench their fist while the ball is in the air. Other actions can be tried – flipping the hand over; making a high-five, and so on.

Tip: For variety, children can try this with their non-dominant hand, or can practise throwing and catching in a controlled way from one hand to the other.

11. Shaken, not stirred

This energizer uses shaking and wriggling to speed up children's circulation and refresh their brains.

What you need: nothing

What to do:

Tell children that they are going to shake and wiggle every part of their body in turn, starting at their head and ending at their toes. Talk children through wiggling their heads, shoulders, arms, wrists, hands, fingers, hips, legs, feet and toes.

12. Activity spellings

In this energizer, children intersperse spelling with movements: a very kinaesthetic form of learning.

What you need: a list of spelling words which children are learning; a piece of paper and pencil for each child or for each pair

What to do:

Children can work in pairs or individually. First, you are going to call out a physical activity for the children to do, and when you call, '*Spell*', they have to stop the activity, listen for the spelling word and write it on their paper as quickly as they can. Then you resume calling the activities until the next word. Activities to call, can include:

- hopping on the left foot
- hopping on the right foot
- clapping hands
- marching on the spot
- running on the spot
- star jumps (if space permits)
- reaching for the stars
- jumping to the left
- jumping to the right.

Tip: This exercise can be carried out with times tables instead of spellings, or by asking children to answer quick questions about topics they are learning.

13. Dancing in the mirror

This energizer involves left-brain/right-brain activity in a fun way that motivates and inspires children.

What you need: nothing

What to do:

Tell children that they are going to pretend to be looking in the mirror whilst dancing using only the top half of their bodies (i.e. not moving their feet); but the 'mirror' is going to be another child.

Divide the children into pairs, each labelled A or B.

Play the dance music while child A leads the dance and child B tries to be the mirror image.

Reverse so that child B leads the dance.

Tip: Once your children have got the hang of this activity, you can introduce dance music. If any of them are having difficulty keeping up with their dancing partner, stop the activity and ask them to say a few words about what is easy to follow and what is difficult.

14. What a stretch

This energizer teaches children that stretching movements are useful between sedentary activities because they improve circulation.

What you need: nothing

What to do:

Make sure the children are not standing too close together. Ask children, while standing, to:

- reach up for the sky
- bend over to flop to the floor
- reach to the right
- reach to the left
- reach out in front
- reach up with their right hand
- reach up with their left hand
- reach down sideways with their right hand
- reach down sideways with their left hand
- shake out their hands and then their feet
- ending with a turn-about.

Tip: You could develop a little routine they could do whilst still sitting down, to minimise disruption between activities. For instance, you could try the exercises now recommended on airlines: circling one foot, then the other; then bending one ankle up and down, then the other; flexing each knee; and so on, moving each part of the body up to the head and down the arms.

15. Mexican wave

This exuberant energizer invigorates everyone whilst strengthening their sense of being part of a positive group.

What you need: nothing

What to do:

Explain to the class that a Mexican Wave is a synchronised, wave-like body movement in one direction of many people moving together.

Ask them whether they have ever seen this movement spread through a crowd, either on television or in real life and, if necessary, ask eight children to come to the front to demonstrate.

See if the class can carry out a wave, either in a circle or in their rows, depending on what formation they are in when they are doing this activity.

Tip: An alternative is to ask the children to 'pass on' a singing note: 'ha' from one to the next along the row. They can do this instead of, or as well as, the wave.

16. What next?

This energizer requires concentration and memory. You demonstrate a movement and the children follow your lead, but always one step behind it.

What you need: nothing

What to do:

Stand in front of the class and begin a repetitive activity, for instance, clapping one hand on the other shoulder. The children watch, and when you change to a new movement (for instance, tapping the top of the head) they must start imitating the first activity.

Each time you change to a new movement, the children take up the one that has just finished, so that they are always one activity behind you. Examples of activities:

- clapping
- walking on the spot
- tapping one foot or the other on the floor
- knocking knees together
- hip wiggling
- shrugging shoulders
- touching both elbows in front
- waving.

17. Good morning, everyone

This energizer helps children build up a movement routine so memory and concentration are involved.

What you need: nothing

What to do:

Call out the movements you want children to perform:

- *Jumping Jacks (x 5)*
- *hop on the left foot (x 5)*
- *hop on the right foot (x 5)*
- *jump feet together, then feet shoulder width apart, then feet together (x 5)*
- *jump with one foot in front of the other, then change feet round and repeat (x 5)*

Adapt these movements according to the space available, or alternate the physical exercises with on-the-spot stretches, such as:

- *reach up to the ceiling (hold for the count of 5)*
- *bend down to touch toes*
- *bring one knee towards the chest, then the other*
- *relax with three deep breaths.*

Children will get used to the routine so you will soon not have to explain every move each time.

18. A nice, long stretch

In this energizer, children pretend they have just woken from a long sleep and stretch their limbs, which gets vitalizing oxygen into their bloodstream.

What you need: nothing

What to do:

In the animal kingdom, many animals wake themselves by stretching their bodies. Ask the children to imagine they have just woken from a long sleep, to stretch up to the ceiling and then stretch their arms out in front of them, to the sides and downwards.

Ask them to sit down, lift their legs and stretch them out, rotate their feet, point their toes, and then relax. Only gentle stretching should be carried out while the muscles are cold, for example, after sitting down for a time.

Tip: Children will be able to think of other stretches. Ask for a volunteer to come to the front to show the others some stretches they have learnt through their favourite sport or from a dance class.

19. Duck, duck, goose

This energizer is more than just physical activity because it requires concentration and quick reactions.

What you need: as much space as possible and a floor that is not slippery

What to do:

Ask the children to sit cross-legged in a wide circle.

All the players sitting in the circle are ducks.

One child is chosen by the teacher to be the fox. The fox walks slowly round the circle, tapping (very lightly) the top of each duck's head, and saying, *'Duck',* with each tap.

After a few moments of this, the fox chooses a goose, by tapping one player's head and calling out, *'Goose!'*

The goose must quickly get up and chase the fox round the circle, trying to 'tag' the fox before the fox reaches the spot where the goose was sitting.

If the fox reaches the goose's place, she is safe and can sit down, and the goose then becomes the fox. If the fox is tagged while running round the circle, start the game again with a new fox.

Tip: Make a tail to go on the fox to make it easier for them to be tagged.

20. Walk this way

Combine physical activity with imagination as children use role play to try out different ways of walking.

What you need: nothing except some space for children to move around

What to do:

Explain to the children that they are to be cartoon characters doing the funniest walk they can.

Or they can try out various ways of walking – like a ballet dancer, for instance; a tightrope walker; walking with a book on the head; walking like a penguin.

This is fun doing this in pairs or groups. They can demonstrate their walk to the rest of the class and the other children can try to guess what they represent.

21. Throw and catch

In this energizer, children develop hand–eye co-ordination and have fun refreshing tired minds and bodies.

What you need: a beanbag or other soft object for each pupil. If children are working in pairs, they will need one object to throw between two.

What to do:

Ask the children to find a space and practise skilful, controlled throwing and catching of their object, counting how many times they can throw and catch, using very small throws into the air, without dropping it. Variations can be:

- throwing and catching with left hand
- throwing and catching with right hand
- throwing with one hand and catching with the other.

Tip: Children may need to be taught and to practise very small throws before this activity is successful.

22. Caught in a storm

In this energizer, children need to be alert and quick off the mark. It stimulates their imaginations whilst exercising their bodies

What you need: space for children to lie down on the floor

What to do:

Ask the children to sit in a space on the floor.

Demonstrate the following instructions:

- row the boat – children to sit on the floor and pretend to row
- man overboard – children lie on their stomachs and pretend to swim
- catch a fish – children stand and pull in a heavy fish
- fish in the boat – children lie on their backs and wriggle
- storm alert – children sit on the floor with head in hands and shiver and shake
- all safe – children lie on their backs, arms outstretched, and relax.

Briskly call out the instructions and ask everyone to respond as quickly as they can.

Tip: Keep everyone alert by changing the order in which you call instructions.

23. Motorbiking

Children must ride imaginary motorbikes without bumping. It combines movement with spatial awareness.

What you need: space for children to move around without bumping into each other

What to do:

Ask the group to raise their arms as if they are holding the handlebars of a motorbike. Then they must move around the space without touching one another.

When they hear the following commands they must react quickly:

- *Start the engine – lift right leg and press down a few times*
- *Right turn – lean to the right*
- *Left turn – lean to the left*
- *Bumpy road – jump up and down*
- *Traffic light – slow down and sit on the floor.*

24. Line them up!

This energizer requires cognitive activity as well as physical exercise.

What you need: a space for the children to line up

What to do:

Divide the class into two groups. Tell each group they must line up as quickly as possible in a certain order that you will ask for. Remind them that it is important for them to work together, to communicate and to be calm when working this out. Also, tell them they will need to be flexible and may need to move several times to achieve your specified order. Try the following ideas:

- in height order
- in alphabetical order of first or last names
- as above but in reverse alphabetical order
- in age order.

25. Best foot forward

In this energizer, children have to cross the room using movements called by the teacher. The movements require balance and control.

What you need: nothing

What to do:

Start with children standing in a space. Explain that they are to move from one side of the room to the other using variously measured paces. Explain that this is not a race. They are to use Tiny, Small or Large movements forward, as follows:

Toes	Moving forward one set of toes ahead of the other toes
Feet	One foot in front of the other foot
Step	One normal small step forward
Stride	One very large pace forward
Jump	One jump forward, with both feet together.

Vary and randomise the steps forward to make it more fun. When children are doing this easily, ask them to vary their direction, going backwards as well as forwards, and from side to side.

26. Foxes and rabbits

In this energizer, the fox must run around the trees in order to catch the rabbit. Speed, agility and control are called for.

What you need: six fabric bands to wear: three in one colour and three in another; space to move about in

What to do:

Choose six children: three to be foxes; three to be rabbits. The rest of the children act as trees in the woods. The aim is for the foxes to catch the rabbits. The trees spread themselves out in the playing area and can move about to shelter the rabbits, and the rabbits can run amongst the trees, to avoid the foxes. The foxes must not touch the trees. Any rabbit that is tagged by a fox must move to one side of the playing area and wait for the end of the game. After a few minutes or when all the rabbits are tagged, change the roles of the children. Remind children that the foxes must not touch the trees at all.

Tip: You can have more rabbits or more foxes to change the balance of the game, and tell the trees they must not move their feet.

Language Energizers

The energizers in this section revive children's vitality with language-based games and activities.

This section includes speaking, listening and written activities to energize the language areas of children's brains. Some are oral, others written, but all are quick, motivating and invigorating. At the same time, they take the academic pressure off children and allow their imagination to flourish.

The selection includes discussion, guessing games, questioning, imaginative and experimental uses of language. These games are particularly good for children with strong verbal and auditory preferences. Above all, they develop children's communication skills.

Giving your class a short break from academic work and allowing them time to indulge in their innate love of wordplay will enliven them so that when you return to more serious matters, they will work with more zest and enthusiasm.

27. Cartoon character

This energizer requires children to draw cartoons. It energizes by restoring an element of fun when children are flagging.

What you need: each child needs a pencil and a piece of paper

What to do:

Ask children to make a brief sketch in the middle of the page, of a character doing some activity. For instance, they might draw a cartoon character skiing, a film star driving or someone they know gardening.

Give them a time limit of, say, two minutes.

Ask the children to draw a bubble coming out of their character's mouth and to write in it what their character is thinking.

28. What am I thinking about?

In this energizer, children question the teacher to find out the mystery item he or she is thinking about.

What you need: an adult's chair at the front of the classroom, facing the class

What to do:

Start by sitting in the hot seat yourself.

Think of something specific – for instance, an object, a country, an animal, or a famous person.

The children must guess, by asking questions, what you are thinking about.
Children with questions must put up their hands and wait to be invited to ask them.

29. One at a time

In this energizer, a child sits in the hot seat and must guess a mystery object from clues given by the class. This is a fun activity but it requires careful thought from everyone.

What you need: an adult's chair at the front of the classroom,
facing the class

What to do:

The child in the hot seat sits with his/her back to the board and must not turn round to see it. You write the name of something – an animal, a country, or whatever is decided – and the class, one at a time, says a sentence about the object without giving away what it is. The child in the hot seat must guess the object from the sentences as quickly as possible.

30. Hobbies

In this energizer, children work together to find out more about each other. This energizes them by widening their social network and making them feel more confident and 'at home' in your setting.

What you need: nothing

What to do:

Pair up the children with someone they don't normally play with, and then ask them to try to discover some outside-school hobbies and interests they both enjoy.

Tip: With very young children ask them to agree on two things they always like to eat.

31. A to Z

This energizer requires children to think hard and use their auditory awareness in an invigorating way.

What you need: nothing

What to do:

Children name animals beginning with each letter of the alphabet from A to Z, for example:

- A   Antelope
- B   Buffalo
- C   Cat
- D   Dog
- E   Elephant
- F   Frog

If there are more children in the class than letters to complete, start again at A when you have reached the end of the alphabet.

32. True, true, false

In this energizer, children write things about themselves. Their classmates turn detective to decide which are true, or false.

What you need: a pencil and a piece of paper for each child

What to do:

Tell each child they must make up three statements about themselves; two true and one false. For example:

- I really like ice-cream.
- My favourite sport is football.
- I can swim five widths of the pool.

Remind them that their false sentence can be placed anywhere in the list. Children then circulate in the classroom, pick a partner and ask questions that will reveal which of each other's statements are the false ones. They continue to circulate, for as long as you like, and to keep a tally of how many they get right.

Tip: Alternatively, ask individual children to come to the front and tell two truths and one lie. The class ask questions to find out which is the lie, and the child at the front does his best to fool the class.

33. Acrostic name poems

This energizer spurs children to think about themselves in positive and imaginative ways.

What you need: a piece of paper and pencil for each child

What to do:

Show children a list on the blackboard of the letters in a name, and explain that you are going to find a complimentary word about that person beginning with each letter. For instance, the name Joe could be:

J – jolly

O – organised

E – energetic.

Ask the children to do this with their own names, using surname as well if the first name is very short.

34. A good bounce

Children bounce a ball and with each bounce think of a positive attribute, helping both physical and emotional well-being.

What you need: a small, soft and bouncy ball

What to do:

Children take turns to think of a positive adjective they think applies to themselves and to say it aloud. As they say it, they bounce the ball once and pass it on to the next child. Examples of positive adjectives:

> Friendly
>
> Helpful
>
> Caring
>
> Fun
>
> Happy.

If this activity moves too slowly, divide the children into small groups with a ball for each group, so that each child's turn comes round more quickly and the concentration span does not need to be so long.

Tip: Children can be asked to think of other things, like an animal that they would be, a plant they like or a country they would like to visit one day. Change the rules, by asking children to bounce the ball from one hand onto the floor and catch it with the other hand, or throw it with one hand and catch it with the other.

35. Nonsense

Children make up nonsense conversations and practise emotional awareness.

What you need: nothing, but a copy of 'Jabberwocky' could be useful

What to do:

Explain to the class that nonsense is talk that is meaningless and incomprehensible. As an example, say something yourself which is nonsense, to make them realise that the tone of voice can make meaningless words meaningful. Say a few nonsense sentences, in an angry voice, a worried voice, a friendly or laughing voice, and ask them to guess what you are saying.

Then ask the children to get into pairs and to have a short nonsense conversation with each other. Remind them to keep their voices fairly low so that other children nearby can hear themselves think. At the end, ask for a few of the favourite nonsense words or ideas that the children came up with.

Tip: Read the poem 'Jabberwocky' (from *Alice Through the Looking Glass*), or some nonsense poems by Edward Lear, either to introduce this activity or after the children have come up with their own words.

36. Finish the phrase

Children use skills of recall to complete well-known advertising slogans.

What you need: nothing

What to do:

Remind the children that they know lots of phrases and ask them whether they can recognise and finish the ones you have started. You can make it competitive. Examples of half-finished sentences:

- Beanz meanz   (Heinz)
- Chick, chick, chick, chick chicken   (lay a little egg for me)
- ET   (phone home)
- Nice to see you   (to see you, nice)
- May the force   (be with you)
- Is it a bird, is it a plane   (no, it's Superman)
- Row, row, row the boat   (gently down the stream)
- Head, shoulders   (knees and toes, knees and toes)
- North, South   (East, West)
- Izzy wizzy   (let's get busy).

Tip: Do this activity verbally, or have the phrases prepared on paper. Children can either complete the unfinished phrases, or match beginnings to ends, or make up their own beginning stems.

37. Words of a letter stick together

Against the clock, children use lateral thinking to say as many words as they can which begin with the same letter.

What you need: an alarm clock

What to do:

Children work in pairs. One of the pair picks a letter from the alphabet and then, for one minute, lists every word he can think of beginning with that letter. The other person in the pair listens and counts the words. After one minute they swap roles. At the end, ask, *Did anyone have over thirty words? Over twenty? Over ten? Over five? Over three? Which letters yielded the most words?*

Tip: For older children, you can make the exercise more challenging by saying they must choose only nouns or adjectives or verbs.

38. Thesaurus

Children must experiment to invent descriptive words.

What you need: paper and pencils

What to do:

The Inuit are said to have many different words for 'snow'. Children could make up their own words for wet snow, powdery snow, hard snow, snow that drifts, snow that is good for making snowballs, etc.

Or ask the children to make up a new word to describe something exciting; for example, the feeling of going down a slide or on a fairground ride. Let them experiment with saying words out loud in pairs and choose a few children at the end to tell the class their word.

Tip: Extend the work by getting children to write a definition of the word and put it into a class dictionary or thesaurus.

39. Persuasion

Children use skills of negotiation and communication to persuade others to do something.

What you need: written on the board, some requests that would require persuasion; for instance:

> *Please give up your seat for me.*
>
> *I would like the last apple in the fruit bowl.*
>
> *I want to buy a new pair of trousers, etc.*

What to do:

Use the examples on the board to discuss with the children how we persuade people: for instance, just asking someone to give up a seat for us may not persuade them to do it, but if we explain that we are feeling poorly or have a bad leg, we may succeed. Sometimes we can persuade people to do us a favour by doing something for them in return.

Ask the children to work in small groups. Give each group a specific scenario: for instance, ask them to pretend that you have only two cinema tickets for a film which every one of the group would like to see. Their task is to make their case, one at a time, for being given one of the tickets. The rest of the class must listen and then vote on who gave the best reasons.

40. Tell me the title

Children use only closed questions to discover the title of a traditional or well-known title.

What you need: titles of traditional stories, books or films that all the children will know

What to do:

Tell the children you are thinking of a book/film/well-known story. The children can ask you questions to find out the title, but you can only answer *Yes* or *No*. Or you can do this with a pair of children at the front of the class, one with the knowledge, the other answering the questions, while the rest of the class listen and can put up their hand when they think they know the answer.

41. The laugh meter

Laughter is a great energizer. Here, children think up jokes and funny stories.

What you need: nothing

What to do:

Ask the children to think how they could cheer up someone who was feeling sad. Give them a few moments to think of jokes, funny faces, little stories or kind words, hugs or a pat on the back. Ask for volunteers to share the joke. Choose a few and let the children award a score on a 'laugh meter' for how funny they are, i.e. they clap softly if only just amused, and very hard if it's rib-tickling!

42. Associations

This is a word-association game which goes around the class.

What you need: nothing

What to do:

Describe to children what word association is, giving them some examples.
For instance: *bacon/eggs; mother/father.*

Ask one child to start by saying a word, and you say back an associated word. Try it again with another child and repeat until all children start to understand what is expected. Then let the game go round the class: for example, a child might start with 'giraffe' and the next child might come up with 'neck'. The aim, of course, is to be very quick and not think too hard about the words. Children can also do this in pairs and have a quick-fire session between the two of them.

Tip: Children can be asked in pairs or groups to do a word association of six words only, and when they reach word number six, the next child in the pair has to try to remember the previous word and work back like that to the original word. This is good for practising recall skills.

43. Fact-finders

Children work together to find out who meets the descriptions you have provided. This activity stimulates curiosity while promoting social skills.

What you need: a photocopy of a pre-printed grid with a few squares on it, with a 'fact mission' written in each square. Either give one grid to each child or ask the class to work in pairs.

What to do:

Children must find someone (or more than one person) to match each 'fact mission' and write their names in the squares. So, they would need to find, for instance, someone in the class who:

- has ever worn socks of different colours
- has a relative in Australia
- has been to the zoo
- has made their own packed lunch
- has one sister
- has had their hair cut within the last two weeks
- says that spaghetti bolognaise is a favourite meal
- is learning to play the piano
- has a guinea-pig as a pet
- will have a birthday within the next month
- knows that most plants need a growing medium (e.g. soil), water and sunshine.

As soon as a child has completed the grid, he or she calls '*BINGO!*'

Tip: You can simplify this by simply reading out your list and ask children to stand up when they have answered yes to, say, three items. Keep going until all are standing.

44. Poem in a triangle

Children create a poem in the shape of a triangle, promoting positive thinking about themselves as members of a group.

What you need: a teacher's board with a pen, or a flip chart sheet with a pen; a pencil; and one piece of paper or rough jotter for each group of children

What to do:

Divide the children into groups of three or four. Explain that they are going to write a 'positive' triangular poem. Demonstrate by writing one on the board. Example:

We
are a
fabulous group.
We can write poems
in a triangular shape and
make them look fantastically good!

Ask the children to create their poem together as a group, with one person chosen to do the writing.

45. Slogan time

Children require creativity and an understanding of persuasive language to invent a product and create a slogan.

What you need: blackboard or whiteboard

What to do:

Tell the children they are all the producers of a fantastic new product that is going to help lots of people. Have a quick think with the children what this new product could be: something fantastical would be best – like a constantly-pouring milk bottle that never runs out, or a light bulb that lights up when it knows you are home. If you are pressed for time, create your own amazing product first, either by telling the children about it or by putting your own label on a plastic bottle or other object. Write children's good ideas on the board. Remind children what slogans for products are and provide some examples (something up-to-date from TV advertising). Then ask the children to think up their own slogan, as if they were going to advertise their new product on television.

46. Snapshots

Children have to break free from stereotypes as they guess the job of people in the photos.

What you need: photos of a variety of people; you need people who do a particular job or activity. Some of these should not be obvious from the photos and try to include some which run against stereotypes – such as athlete, Tanni Grey Thompson, or musician, Nigel Kennedy.

What to do:

Display these pictures where the children can see them well. Display labels such as athlete, musician, etc. Ask children in groups to try to work out what they think these people do. Ask each group to share their findings on one of their photos and explain how they made their choices. Then tell them the truth and see whether you have managed to shatter some stereotypical illusions!

47. Mini language lesson

Using other languages really gets the brain going.

What you need: some words in languages other than their own. (You might get assistance from a parent or member of staff with a different mother tongue to record these words for you.) Choose simple familiar words or phrases, such as 'hello', 'goodbye', 'please', 'thank you', 'my name is', and so on.

What to do:

Let the children listen to the words and phrases, telling them the name of the language and showing on an atlas where it is spoken. Give them practice in saying the words. Children in your class may be delighted to share their own knowledge of non-English words.

Imaginative Energizers

The energizers in this section invigorate children through activities that allow them the freedom to open their minds and make unexpected and unusual connections.

Our imaginations are places where the impossible can happen and there is no limit on what just might happen. All creative thought – artistic and scientific – requires an agile and zestful imagination, and all children need to have space in their lives to let them exercise this crucial aspect of human activity because it is a place where we find reasons to motivate and animate ourselves.

In this section, children need to use their imaginations to come up with creative and inventive ways to complete simple, entertaining tasks. Some are designed to encourage different modes of self-expression; others pose mental challenges that stimulate their minds and motivate them to think hard and fast.

Activities like these give children a burst of opportunity to try out new ideas and new ways of thinking, safe in the knowledge that these brief activities are planned to be friendly and good humoured.

48. Olympic gold

In this energizer, children have to mime a sport. They need to engage their minds and take physical action.

What you need: nothing

What to do:

Ask your children to stand at their desk or in a space and point out to them the variety of actions that sportsmen and sportswomen do. Ask them to mime and pretend they are doing a few of these sports activities for just a few seconds.

- riding a horse in a race
- scoring a try in rugby
- doing a winning serve in tennis
- driving a Formula 1 car in a race
- mountain biking through a wood
- cross-country running
- playing table tennis
- trampolining.

49. Cooking up a feast

This energizer helps children revive themselves through their senses whilst miming the preparation of food and imagining its taste and smell.

What you need: nothing

What to do:

Tell the children they are going to mime cooking up a birthday feast or making a fabulous picnic. Tell children to mime the following for just a few seconds and to imagine they can smell the food while they are doing it:

- mixing up a cake
- icing a cake
- making sandwiches
- washing tomatoes
- putting biscuits on a plate
- cutting up apples
- frying sausages.

50. On the farm

When they engage in this energizer, children think about a completely different environment as they mime work on the farm.

What you need: nothing: city children may need to discuss some of these things first – they may have no idea about milking cows

What to do:

Tell the children they are going to mime some jobs on the farm. Ask them to mime each of these activities – if they have no experience of farm life, you may have to demonstrate and they can copy you:

- patting the farm dog
- grooming a cart horse
- milking a cow
- shearing the sheep
- feeding the hens
- collecting the hens' eggs
- taking the goat for a walk
- driving the tractor.

Children start by doing one activity (perhaps, feeding the hens). Then, when you call for the next one, they carry on doing the previous activity with one hand and do the next activity with the other hand – so now they may be feeding the hens with one hand and milking a cow with another. When a third activity is called, they stop the first activity and do the third with that hand.

51. It's a tough job!

To succeed in this energizer, children need to engage observation skills to act out the jobs in various types of employment.

What you need: nothing

What to do:

Tell the children they are going to mime doing different people's jobs. Ask children to mime the following for just a few seconds:

- building a house
- working at a shop till
- driving a lorry
- cutting hair
- cutting the grass
- word processing at a PC
- mending a car
- being a dentist.

Ask children to do one activity with one hand and another with the other hand. When you call out each job, children mime the activity of the last job you called, not the current one. So, if you call out 'builder', followed by 'hairdresser', the children mime building while you call for hairdressing – and so on.

52. On the stage

This energizer uses positive thinking to give children a boost as they imagine a scene in which their success is celebrated.

What you need: nothing

What to do:

Ask children to sit with their hands in their laps, shutting their eyes. Tell them to imagine that they are in a crowded assembly hall with a large stage at the front. Allow a moment for them to create this image, and continue:

> *Someone is giving a super prize to a pupil and, when you look, you see that the pupil is you. Imagine that you are on the stage and you are being given a super prize. When you look out into the audience, everyone is clapping and cheering, and you can see family, friends and teachers all cheering for you, all happy for you in your achievements. Imagine something that you have done well, or a time when you made someone happy – something people might want to celebrate. Just enjoy that moment of pride and pleasure.*
>
> *(Pause.)*
>
> *Now you are going to 'come back to the classroom', open your eyes, have a big stretch and take a few nice big breaths.*

53. At the fairground

This energizer encourages children to engage their senses to 'experience' a fairground ride.

What you need: nothing

What to do:

Ask children to sit with their hands in their laps, shutting their eyes. Tell them to imagine that they are going as a treat to a fairground. Follow or adapt the script below:

> *You arrive at the fairground and you can see lots of people. You can smell the grass under your feet and, in the air, the candy-floss being made. You walk past exciting stalls with balls to throw, prizes to win, children enjoying themselves. You get to your favourite roundabout or fairground ride and pay your money. You sit tight and fasten your seatbelt. The ride starts; you feel safe and happy, going round, the wind in your hair, people laughing and happy all around you. Eventually, the ride comes to a halt. You unfasten your seatbelt and to go back to your family and friends to tell them what it was like.*
>
> (Pause.)
>
> *Now it is time to 'come back to the classroom', to wiggle your fingers and toes, take a couple of nice deep breaths and open your eyes.*

54. At the match

This energizer demonstrates to children that success is a great way to add verve to our lives.

What you need: nothing

What to do:

Ask children to sit with their hands in their laps and shut their eyes. Tell them that they are going to use their imaginations to go on a little journey to watch a sports game. Follow or adapt the script below:

> *You are very excited today as you are going to watch your favourite sport. You decide whether it's a football match, swimming race, horse-riding competition, gymnastics or trampoline display. As you arrive, you can see lots of people waiting to cheer the competition or match. You can see all the people who are going to take part getting ready, warming up and preparing, and suddenly the sport starts. You see them playing an excellent game or giving a great display. You feel safe and happy watching from the sidelines and start to cheer them all on.*
>
> (Pause.)
>
> *You watch for a little bit longer, then give a final cheer and realise it is time to 'come back to the classroom'. Wiggle your fingers and toes, take a couple of nice deep breaths and gently open your eyes and look around the room. Give your neighbour a smile.*

55. Ice magic

This energizer prompts children to try to capture the sensations of learning to skate successfully.

What you need: nothing

What to do:

Ask children to sit with their hands in their laps, shutting their eyes. Tell them that they are going to use their imaginations to go to an ice-skating rink. Follow or adapt the script below:

> *Today is a special day. You are going to an ice-skating rink with your friends, and you are very happy about this because you have been looking forward to it for a long time. As you arrive at the rink with your friends, you put on your special skating boots and walk over to the ice. You can almost smell the ice before you step onto it. You find you can start skating quite well. Start by going carefully along by the side, and when you have practised for a while and are beginning to feel confident, you can move into the middle of the rink. It is very exciting now, to skate in the middle with your friends, going faster, but still feeling safe and in control of where you are going. Practise your skills on ice for a little longer – imagine skating backwards or doing some twirls and spins. Imagine all the good feelings this brings you…*
>
> *(Pause.)*
>
> *Now it is time to come back into your classroom. Wiggle your fingers and toes, take a couple of nice deep breaths and gently open your eyes and look around the room. Have a good stretch.*

56. The bottomless suitcase

In this energizer, children entertain each other by miming what they have found in a suitcase.

What you need: nothing

What to do:

Mime, for the children, the actions of carrying a big, heavy suitcase and putting it down at the front of the classroom. Choose a child to go to the 'suitcase' and to pretend to take out an object. The pupil decides what the object is but does not tell anyone. The child demonstrates using the object and the others have to guess what it is: for example, a tennis racquet, Wellington boots, a bicycle or an umbrella.

57. Super heroes

This energizer offers a positive use for our imaginations, as children share their ways to save the planet.

What you need: nothing

What to do:

Tell the children to pretend that a meteor is heading towards the earth.

They, and their partner next to them, are a superhero team. The children can choose which superheroes to be. Give them a few minutes to devise a plan to save the world.

Ask pairs of children who have been working co-operatively and listening to each other to tell the class their plan, however out of this world it may be!

58. What am I doing now?

This works as an instant energizer to re-engage children's interest by asking them to guess just what you are doing!

What you need: nothing

What to do:

Make sure all children can see what you are doing. Mime some different actions and ask the children to guess what you are doing. For instance:

- peel a banana
- play some shots with a tennis racquet
- hammer a nail
- throw a ball
- brush your teeth
- drive a car
- cycle on your bike.

Ask one of the children to stand at the front and lead the activity. Alternatively, ask two children to mime something together, like playing catch, making a cake, building a sand castle.

59. The ele-cat-cow-fox

This energizer harnesses the power of imagination and asks children to create an animal hybrid.

What you need: a piece of paper and pencil for each child

What to do:

Tell the children to think of a four-legged animal and to put the piece of paper lengthways in front of them. Ask them to draw the head of an animal, with a neck, on the left-hand side of the paper about half way up. They must not tell anyone what their animal is.

Children then fold over the head they have drawn and pass on the paper to their neighbour (each child passing the paper in the same direction). Only a little bit of the neck should be visible to the next person.

 Ask the children then to draw the front legs and half the tummy of any four-legged animal on the piece of paper passed to them, then fold it over and pass it on, leaving just the middle of the tummy visible.

The next drawing is of the hind-quarters of an animal, with just the last bit of its rump showing for the next person when the paper is folded. The last drawing is of an animal's tail. When the last person has drawn this, they pass it on once more.

Then, all the papers are opened to see what the completed animals are. Children will be keen to see the animals they have contributed to, so ask them to pass the papers back down the row for a mutual giggle.

60. Squiggling

This energizer stimulates children through their hands and eyes as they 'take a line for a walk'.

What you need: a piece of paper; pencil or pen; and colours for each child

What to do:

Ask each child to draw on their piece of paper with their pen or pencil, carefully, without taking the pen off the paper until the paper is quite patterned. You can show them on a board or flip chart what you mean.

Keeping their own patterns or swapping with neighbours, children then look at their patterns carefully for four minutes, finding and shading in as many well-known objects or animals as they can in the pattern.

At the end, see who could find the most objects in their pattern.

61. Birthday party

In this energizer, children use fantasy to dream up their ideal birthday party.

What you need: nothing

What to do:

Explain to the children that they are having an imaginary birthday and they can have any type of party they want. Ask them to think of ideas for their party. Share the party ideas, either by asking each child in turn, or by asking them to explain their ideas briefly to their neighbours.

62. If I had a magic wand

Children are revitalized by deciding what to do with a magic wand.

What you need: a piece of paper and a pencil

What to do:

Ask the children to imagine they have magic wand, which keeps its magic for only five minutes. They must think of what they would do with their magic wand, write it and/or draw a quick thumbnail sketch to illustrate it.

After five minutes, stop the children, since the magic has run out, and ask them to share with a neighbour what they have written or drawn.

Read out all, or a selection of, the wishes, and ask the class to discuss them and to vote for the best wish.

Tip: You might want to give a special commendation to those children whose wishes help other people.

63. Desert island

This energizer stimulates children's reasoning and problem-solving skills in a gratifying way.

What you need: a piece of paper or rough jotter and pencil for each child

What to do:

Tell the children to imagine they have been shipwrecked on a desert island. Their only possession is a suitcase, containing five items that will be useful.

Ask the children to decide what these items are and to draw them. When they have finished doing this, they can explain their choices to a neighbour or with the class.

Tip: You might vary the categories for the items, or the number of items; for example, only comforting items that remind them of home, or only items that will aid survival, or be useful in a medical emergency.

64. Paper sculpture

This energizer gives children free reign to imagination to create something interesting and unique.

What you need: a sheet of A4 paper for each child

What to do:

Give the children a short amount of time to find words and pictures that represent for them some good things in life. They then cut or tear out their selected pictures or words and use them to make a collage on their piece of paper.

At the end, ask a child in each row or on each table to go round with a bin or bag to collect rubbish and glues. Keep what is left of magazines, for future use, so that pictures can be added to or completed in other sessions.

65. Newspaper animals

This energizes children with ingenuity as a pep-me-up.

What you need: sheets of newspaper, at least one for each pupil. Bin or bag for the waste.

What to do:

Give each child a large sheet of newspaper. Ask them to tear the paper to make an animal. Giving a time limit of two or three minutes will help to focus their minds. After this time, children can hold up their animals for the rest of the class to see.

As this exercise can make a mess, ask all children to put their waste paper on their table in front of them then ask one child from each row or table to collect the waste from that table or row in a bag or box for recycling.

Tip: A variant is to give them a piece of paper, glue and newspaper and ask them to make a picture out of torn-up bits of newspaper (e.g. a black and white cat; a tree in winter).

66. Paper planes

This energizer encourages children to feel the joy of being inventive.

What you need: a sheet of paper for each pupil

What to do:

Tell the children that their goal is to make a paper plane. Give them a short, limited time to make their planes.

Choose a few of the most convincing-looking or the most original designs and ask their creators to show them and describe a wonderful journey in their plane.

Tip: It is hard for children to resist throwing their planes, but this can cause chaos in the classroom. So do the activity outside if you can, or in the hall, or do it just before playtime so that the children can take them into the playground.

67. A crooked tale

In this energizer, children have the novel experience of drawing with their eyes shut and feel animated by the experience.

What you need: paper and pencil or pen for each child

What to do:

Divide the children into groups of four. Ask one child in each group to draw a man whilst keeping their eyes shut. Ask another to draw a house, one to draw a cat and one to draw a mouse. All must keep their eyes shut throughout. They can then put the drawings together to represent the nursery rhyme, and draw a crooked line to link all four.

> *There was a crooked man who walked a crooked mile.*
> *He found a crooked sixpence upon a crooked style.*
> *He bought a crooked cat that caught a crooked mouse,*
> *And they all lived together in a little crooked house.*

Get them to show their drawings to the class while they all say the rhyme.

Tip: For a slightly longer activity, let each child divide their paper into four and draw all four items.

68. The other half

In this energizer, children wake up the spatial part of their brains by completing a half-made picture.

What you need: photocopies of half-pictures, with the other half of the paper left blank. Try to find action pictures or funny ones; symmetrical pictures are easier. Provide pencils or colours for each child.

What to do:

Give each of the children a photocopied half-picture. Ask them to draw the other half of the picture as precisely as they can.

Tip: This can be a good art activity if you take a portrait picture of each child with a digital camera and then give them half a face.

69. Good things in life

In this energizer, children create a positive atmosphere with a collage representing the good things in life.

What you need: a piece of A4 card and glue for each child. Ask children to bring in one or two finished-with magazines with pictures in. (Collect some yourself in case some children cannot manage this.) Make sure each child has a magazine.

What to do:

Ask children to flick through the pictures and words to see what images and words make them feel good. They can then tear out the pictures and glue them onto their sheet. They can make an attractive montage of feel-good images.

70. Puzzle

This energizer prompts children to use their motor and spatial skills and achieve a pleasurable result.

What you need: a square of card and a pair of appropriate scissors for each child. Ideally, make the card squares of mixed colours.

What to do:

Give each child a square of card and let them create a puzzle by cutting up their square of card into several pieces. They then swap their muddled-up puzzle with their neighbour and the children compete to see how quickly they can put the puzzle back together.

To make things fair, agree in advance with the children how many pieces they are to cut the puzzle into. Suggest to the children that they draw their patterns before cutting them out.

Tip: The puzzles can easily become more complicated, especially for older children, by increasing the size of the card and the number of pieces. Children could also use the pieces to create a form, as in tangrams.

71. Three-minute puppet show

This energizer encourages children to work together to put on a simple puppet show.

What you need: puppets and something like a large cardboard box, which the children can duck behind to give a quick puppet show

What to do:

The group who are going to perform their little show will probably need to know in advance, to give them time to plan their show and be ready: give them a few minutes to do this while the rest of the class continue with whatever they are doing. Make sure the group positions themselves to perform their play where everyone can see and hear them.

Tip: When they are practised at puppetry, ask your class to prepare a little show based on some classroom or school topic of interest to fit in with the broader curriculum, and perform it for other classes.

72. Ten-minute challenge

This energizer works by giving teams a challenge, which they work on co-operatively. This raises their sense of belonging and makes them feel supported and happy.

What you need: children will need to be arranged into small challenge teams. Each group will need the same materials, which can vary according to the challenge. You can start with a newspaper, paperclips, a lump of modelling plastic, a piece of string, or some cotton wool. Other ideas could include pipe cleaners, sticky tape, card, coloured pens or pencils, wool, shiny paper, glue, etc.

What to do:

The team's task is to construct something out of the materials they have been given: for example, a rocket. Let the children work together with the materials that they have been given, with a time limit.

Musical Energizers and Clapping Games

The activities in this section invigorate children through the magic of rhythm and melody. Music is a shared activity that brings us all together and develops a sense of community. This is why we have global traditions of using clapping, chanting and singing to speed up work or enliven repetitive activities.

Here we include singing, clapping games and many simple ways to make sound. Musical activities have the effect of energizing children and making them feel happy and relaxed. Anyone can join in, whatever their level of musical ability. Shy children do not need to feel conspicuous, and boisterous children can let themselves go with gusto, and everyone has the opportunity to 'let it all out' in a controlled and emotionally safe way.

Children love anything that is musical or rhythmic, and these activities help them to learn how to concentrate and listen attentively and develop personal and social skills by working in pairs or as part of a group that is focused on the pleasure of making interesting sounds.

These activities will particularly appeal to children with a strong auditory preference.

73. Clap out, clap in

In this energizer, children clap and make alternating movements.

What you need: nothing

What to do:

Explain to the children that they are going to follow your lead with this clapping rhyme until they have learnt it. Once the children can follow your lead confidently, the teacher can speed up the sequence.

Clap out	(clap with arms stretched out in front)
Clap in	(clap with arms close to the body)
Clap out	(clap with arms stretched out in front)
Clap in	(clap with arms close to the body)
Clap under	(clap UNDER right leg)
Clap over	(clap OVER right leg)
Clap under	(clap UNDER left leg)
Clap over	(clap OVER left leg)
Clap above here	(clap hands above head right-hand side)
Clap above there	(clap hands above head left-hand side)
Clap above here	(clap hands above head right-hand side)
Clap above there	(clap hands above head left-hand side)
And clap,	
Clap	
Clap	
Around	(turn around on the spot).

74. Clap with me

This energizer peps up children with claps and rhythm that is maintained by your guidance.

What you need: nothing

What to do:

Form the circle and explain to the children that they are going to clap some rhythms. At the same time, you are going to call out instructions that they must follow; for example:

> *Clap high* (clap above your head) *1, 2, 3, 4*
>
> *Clap low* (clap down by your knees) *1, 2, 3, 4*
>
> *Clap to the right, 1, 2, 3, 4*
>
> *Clap to the left, 1, 2, 3, 4*
>
> *Clap with your partner* (both hands together) *1, 2, 3, 4.*

You can think up some more complex clapping rhythms or speed up your activity.

75. At the bottom of the sea

In this energizer, children use finger movement and clapping to tell a story about a whale.

What you need: nothing

What to do:

Teach the children the following clapping game.

<u>Clapping key</u>
(ST – Slap Thigh)   (C – Clap hands together)

At the bottom of the sea so blue and   green
Crouch down and touch the floor, ST, C, ST, C.

Is the biggest,   fattest whale   you ever have seen.
Raise arms high and then wide, ST, C, ST, C.

He opens wide his mouth from nose to chin
Open arms like a big mouth, point to nose, point to chin.
And all the little silver fish swim right in.
ST, C, ST, C, wiggle fingers like little fish swimming.

Tip: Children can make up their own extra lines for this clapping rhyme, and their own actions, either as a class with the teacher as scribe on the board, or in pairs using paper. The teacher can choose a child to stand at the front and lead the activity.

76. Class song

In this energizer, children come together to celebrate their sense of community.

What you need: one large whiteboard and markers, or one large piece of flip chart paper

What to do:

Tell the children that you think the class deserves its own song and that they are going to choose a tune to use that they all know. Get the children to come up with some positive things they want to say about their class and use their ideas to write a first verse. Then have fun singing it.

Tip: This can be put to one side and worked on whenever there is a spare moment to refine the verse and to write other verses, until a whole little class song is ready, for singing all together at the end of the day.

77. Body music

In this energizer, you conduct while your children really enjoy using their bodies as sound-makers.

What you need: nothing; or a tuneful CD

What to do:

The children are going to make sounds by using their bodies. Let them work in small groups and either direct them to make a particular sound, or let them choose one sound which their group will make.

For example, make a 'pop' with their lips, clap their hands, swish their palms together, stamp their feet, whistle.

Once these sounds are agreed, give them a few moments to practise.

Then you act as 'conductor', pointing to each group in turn and asking them to 'play' their sounds.

You can either do this without accompaniment, or to act as a percussion accompaniment to a recorded tune.

Tip: It would be fun to accompany a rap poem, either from a book or one which children themselves have written.

78. England, Ireland, Scotland and Wales

This energizer is based on the parts of the British Isles, and alternates high, low, left and right stretches.

What you need: nothing

What to do:

Teach the children the following clapping activity.

England	*Ireland*	*Scotland*	*Wales*
(Clap RIGHT)	(Clap LEFT)	(Clap HIGH)	(Clap LOW)

Up in the hills   *and*   *down in the dales*
(Clap above head 4 times)   (Clap down low 4 times)

Mountains,	*lakes,*	*woodland,*	*vales*
Clap	Clap	Clap	Clap

England	*Ireland*	*Scotland*	*Wales*
(Clap RIGHT)	(Clap LEFT)	(Clap HIGH)	(Clap LOW)

79. I'm happy!

This energizer is a clapping rhyme based on the routines of the day and includes mime.

What you need: nothing

What to do:

Teach children the following clapping game.

I'm	happy (Clap)	happy (Clap)	happy (Clap)	in the morning (STRETCH)
I'm	happy (Clap)	happy (Clap)	happy (Clap)	in the night (MIME SLEEPING)
I'm	happy (Clap)	happy (Clap)	happy (Clap)	when I eat my lunch (MIME EATING)
And	I'm happy (Clap)	happy (Clap)	happy (Clap)	when I write (MIME WRITING)
I'm	happy (Clap)	happy (Clap)	happy (Clap)	in the sunshine (MAKE A BIG SUN WITH ARMS)
I'm	happy (Clap)	happy (Clap)	happy (Clap)	in the rain (wiggle fingers to make rain)
I'm	happy (Clap)	happy (Clap)	happy (Clap)	when I come to school (MIME WALKING TO SCHOOL)
I'm	happy (Clap)	to go (Clap)	home (Clap)	again (MIME WALKING HOME AGAIN)

80. Clap my name

Use children's names to create rhythms, as energizers, which has the added benefit of helping spelling.

What you need: nothing

What to do:

Tell the children they are going to clap the rhythm of their own name, using first name and surname, with one clap per syllable. Work through some examples all together until they get the hang of it. Going along the class, one row at a time, each child claps and says his or her own name. The other children in the row stand up and listen; then, all together, they copy the clapping for that person's name. Then move on to the next person in the row.

Tip: Clap football club names as if you were supporters at a match.

81. Clapping adjectives

In this energizer, children choose adjectives to describe themselves and clap out their names.

What you need: nothing

What to do:

Tell children to think of an adjective to go in front of their own first name, to tell us something about them.

Then all they have to do is:

1. tap their shoulders on 'I am'
2. clap their hands to the syllables of their adjective
3. tap their thighs with the syllables of their name.

Like this:

I am (tap, tap) *spor-ty* (clap, clap) *Sam* (tap).

I am (tap, tap) *kind* (clap) *Kirs-ty* (tap, tap).

Then each child can take a turn at clapping their name.

82. Name that song

This energizer demonstrates that a little competitiveness can be stimulating. Children hum the first few notes of a song, which others then try to guess.

What you need: nothing

What to do:

Hold a little singing competition, with volunteers coming to the front to hum or sing the first few notes of a well-known song. Other children put their hands up as soon as they can guess what the song is.

Whoever gets it right has the chance to come to the front to sing the next song. You can make it more complicated by telling the children to sing only five notes, and see if the others can guess. If they cannot, then they can sing a few more notes.

83. Ring, ring telephone

This energizer can be chanted by small groups and enlivens everyone with the joy of participation.

What you need: nothing

What to do:

Teach children the following singing game. Once the children have learnt it, continue with different names.

> *Ring, ring, telephone, who is there?*
> *Leon's calling Edwin, can you hear?*
> *Pick up the telephone and hear him say,*
> *'Hello Edwin, have a good day!'*

Two names are chosen for the second line. All the children sing the first three lines together, and then the 'caller' sings the final line to the second child chosen.

84. Human beat box

This energizer helps different groups of children enliven themselves as they orchestrate a popular song.

What you need: a recording of a popular song that the children will like

What to do:

Divide the children into groups, or the class into quarters.

Allocate each group a different sound to make; for example, 'boom-boom', 'cha, cha, cha' or 'ting-a-ling'.

Ask the children to watch for when you point to their group (sometimes you'll be pointing to two groups at once).

The children can make these sounds act as an accompaniment to a favourite song that is playing in the background and providing the melody, or they can try to reproduce the tune themselves.

85. Move to the music

Children create movement patterns to convey the mood of a piece of music.

What you need: a music player and recordings of music with a strong, definite beat

What to do:

Ask the children to listen carefully to the music once through, thinking what actions would be appropriate for the different bits of the piece. Play the tune again, asking children to move about the room without touching each other, matching the strength and flow of their movements to the mood of the music. To start the children off, you could explain that they can march to some parts of the music and float, skip or tiptoe to other parts, until they discover their own interpretation.

Tip: African Party CD (Putamayo label) is very good as it's got a strong beat and infectiously happy rhythms.

86. Guess that sound

This energizer uses familiar sounds to sharpen children's listening skills.

What you need: a selection of items that make a noise, like a tambourine, a box of matches, a bunch of keys, a cereal packet, a rattle, a mouth organ

What to do:

This game can be played in a circle or with children in their seats.

All you have to do is make sounds with your objects while the children sit with their eyes shut and try to guess what the sounds are.

Tip: More interesting noises can be produced if they are taped in advance: for example, the sound of children in the playground, the sound of vacuuming or a baby crying.

87. Double, double this, double, double that

This energizer is a rousing clapping rhyme that children do in mirrored pairs, working with concentration and co-ordination.

What you need: nothing

What to do:

Teach the children the following clapping game:

<u>Clapping Key</u>

Fists – 2 people facing each other – double fists, clap together
Flat hands front – 2 people facing each other – both hands flat, clap together in front
Flat hands back – 2 people facing each other – clap backs of both hands in front

Double (Fists)	*Double* (Fists)	*This* (Flat hands front)	
Double (Fists)	*Double* (Fists)	*That* (Flat hands back)	
Double (Fists)	*This* (Flat hands clap front)	*Double* (Fists)	*That* (Flat hands clap back)
Double (Fists)	*Double* (Fists)	*This* (Flat hands clap front)	*That* (Flat hands clap back)

Tip: Vary the speed of this clapping game; it gets livelier as the children do it more quickly. For fun, ask the children if they can do this standing on one leg.

88. Who's in my group?

Children must listen carefully during this energizer and hold a tune in their heads as they search out a partner humming the same thing.

What you need: select five or six songs, write the titles on slips of paper and make enough slips to give out one per child

What to do:

Shuffle the slips of paper and hand them out one per child, asking them not to show each other what is on theirs. Children then move about the classroom humming or singing their song until they find someone else who is singing the same song. They then link arms and walk round singing it together until they have the whole group. By the end of the activity, there should be several groups of singing children. Examples of songs for this could be:

- Twinkle, twinkle little star
- Old Macdonald had a farm
- Row, row, row the boat
- Nursery rhymes for younger children
- Songs that the children know and like from assembly

Tip: You could play this game with topics other than songs: for instance, with the noises of animals (the children mooing, barking, miaowing, clucking, and so on), or with a selection of moods for the children to express happy, sad, scared, excited.

89. Clap your hands, jump up

In this energizer, lots of physical energy can be generated by this song with clapping and actions.

What you need: nothing

What to do:

Teach your group the words of this chant and allow them to make up appropriate actions.

Clap your hands, turn around, jump up high, then touch the ground.
Let's all sing together and make good sound.

Coming in, going out, whisper soft, yell a shout.
Let's all sing and make good sound.

Wave your hands, stamp your feet, march like soldiers to the beat.
Let's all sing and make good sound.

Sing at day, sing at night, sing in dark, sing in light.
Let's all sing and make good sound.

Clap your hands, turn around, jump up high, then touch the ground.
Let's all sing and make good sound.

90. Mr Flibbery Flobbery Flan

Children are energized by 'nonsense' and will have fun thinking up weird and wonderful ways to represent the items in this song.

What you need: nothing

What to do:

Help the children to chant the following song:

Verse One:
*Mr Flibbery Flobbery Flan came from Ala-kazala-kaban
And the clothes that he wore
Were the strangest you ever saw.*

Verse Two:
*Mr Flibbery Flobbery Flan came from Ala-kazala-kaban
And the food that he ate
Was the strangest on any plate.*

Verse Three:
*Mr Flibbery Flobbery Flan came from Ala-kazala-kaban
And the pets that he had
Were considered to be quite mad.*

The children sing items at the end of each verse to represent the strangest clothes, food or pets; the more weird and wonderful the better.

For instance, they may think of a hat made out of jelly or a scarf made out of snake skins; for the food verse, the food could be fried daisies with pumpkin sauce or chocolate worms with fishy ice-cream; and the pets could be a dog with six legs, a high-jumping fish or a jellyfish wearing rubber boots.

91. Grumpy giants

In this energizer, everyone is involved in a chase game that involves words, rhythm and movement.

What you need: nothing

What to do:

Place the children in a circle and teach them to chant the following words:

> *I am at the palace waiting for the king*
> *To give me a ball of yellow skipping string.*
> *Along comes a giant, grumpy and tall*
> *And chases me round the pointy palace wall.*

The children sing or chant this song standing in a circle, facing inwards. They then join hands and raise their arms to form the pointy palace wall. A child is chosen to skip inside the ring while the lines are chanted. At the end of the verse, point to one child and call 'Giant'.

Both children leave the circle and run around the outside in opposite directions, returning to the centre through the space left.

The last child back becomes the skipper. After two turns, choose someone new.

Brain Energizers

This section is particularly about mental stimulation. There is a wide variety of activities but their common element is that they appeal to a whole variety of thinking skills. The section ends with ten mathematical challenges to appeal to children who are stimulated by number work.

Quick-fire challenge gets everyone's attention and perks everyone up. Quizzes and puzzles never fail to attract children's curiosity and spark their interest and those all-important brain cells. They also allow children to relax a little and stretch their brains in a less academic way than usual.

The challenges included here take little time to organize and will brighten the mood in your classroom in no time at all. Competition, used carefully, can be a great motivator. It isn't necessary to set children against each other – many of the challenges here can be set for individuals to measure themselves against, or as challenges for groups to work on together.

92. Drawing on your back

This energizer turns sensation into visualization. It intrigues children and relaxes them at the same time.

What you need: nothing

What to do:

Ask children to pretend that their forefinger is a big felt tip pen. Each child is to draw a number or a letter on a neighbour's back. The child who is being 'drawn' on has to try to guess what the letter or number was.

93. One to ten

In this energizer, children count round in a circle, sometimes leaving out a chosen number.

What you need: nothing

What to do:

This game is fast and is best carried out in a circle, although you may well be able to arrange it in another format, depending upon your classroom set up.

Ask the children to count out loud from one to ten, saying a number each. When a child says 10, the next child starts again at 1. The children will need to practise this to become fluent at it. See how quickly they can do this, and emphasise the need to listen and be ready.

When children have grasped this, introduce a new element, by choosing for one number – for instance, 4 – to be not actually spoken. The child who would have said 4 remains quiet and the counting skips past that child, those either side saying 3 and 5. Try this with other 'silent' numbers, such as odd numbers or even numbers or prime numbers.

94. Who was it?

In this energizer, children look for clues to work out which child took a toy from behind their back.

What you need: a small object; for example, a small toy

What to do:

Choose one child to come to the front of the class and, facing the front, to stand and hold an object in their hands behind their back. Silently point to someone to come up behind the child, take the object and carry it back to his/her seat. Give the child at the front the 'all-clear' and ask him or her to take three guesses at which child took the object. They will try to guess by seeing who looks as if they may be holding the object or who is looking smug.

Tip: You can make this more exciting by using a noisy object like a bunch of keys or a tambourine. Children need to be careful, when they take the object and make their way back to their seat, that the person at the front does not hear which way they went.

95. Tables buzz

This mathematical energizer requires children to count and substitute the word Buzz for chosen multiples, which requires concentration.

What you need: nothing

What to do:

Tell the children that they are going to count round the class, and whenever they come across a number from a certain times table, the child that would have said that number says '*buzz*' instead. For example, with the three times table, the first child would say '*one*', the second child would say '*two*', the third child would say '*buzz*', the fourth child would say '*four*', the fifth child would say '*five*' and the sixth child would say '*buzz*'.

96. Fizz buzz

This energizer is like the previous activity, but involves two sets of tables – and even more concentration.

What you need: nothing

What to do:

All the class stand at their desks or in a ring and count round the class. When the number is a multiple of three, the child whose turn it is says '*fizz*' (e.g. one, two, fizz). When it is a multiple of five the child says '*buzz*' (one, two, fizz, four, buzz). If it is a multiple of both, the child says '*fizz-buzz*' (11, fizz, 13, 14, fizz-buzz, 16).

Tip: Can be played with other multiples.

97. Make a number

This energizer challenges children to make a total from a limited choice of numbers.

What you need: nothing (two dice, optional)

What to do:

Write a number on the board. Randomly select five numbers between one and ten by asking five children to pick a number, or throw dice. Children must then race to make a sum, using only those numbers picked, which make the total on the board. For example: find the total 76, using only the numbers 1, 3, 4, 7, 8.

Tip: Set conditions which suit the ability range of your children, such as 'you can only add and subtract' or 'see how close you can get using each number only once'. When children are familiar with this activity, they can play on their own in small groups.

98. Bull's-eye

This energizer helps children to understand trebles, doubles and single units to work down from 301.

What you need: paper and pencil. Calculator (optional)

What to do:

Start with 301. Using only numbers up to ten (or up to 20 – you can set your own top limit), the children must work out how many darts they must throw to make the number 301, using trebles, doubles and singles. The aim is to use as few as possible. Children can compare results and check each others' sums with a calculator.

99. Fibonacci sequence

This energizer is a challenge for individual children and helps them to enjoy the experience of number patterns.

What you need: children need a piece of paper each and a pencil

What to do:

This sequence, which starts with 0, 1, 1, 2, 3, 5, 8, 13 is formed by adding each number to the one that preceded it in the sequence. This is how it works:

$$0+1=1$$
$$1+1=2$$
$$2+1=3$$
$$3+2=5$$
$$5+3=8$$
$$8+5=13$$

Children can keep the sequence on a piece of paper and add to it when they have a few moments to spare, seeing how far they can get.

If more than one child is doing this, they can compare their answers as they go.

Tip: The Fibonacci sequence can be found in nature and provides a fascinating topic for the mathematically-minded child.

100. Silly jelly!

This energizer invites children to invoke their senses as they get hit by the silly jelly!

What you need: nothing

What to do:

Explain to the children that they are going to have fun with some imaginary green jelly that they will pretend has been thrown over them. They are to mime what it would feel like to have it thrown at them, and pull it off their faces making slurpy and squelching noises.

One child is chosen to start with the imaginary jelly, which he pretends to throw at someone else whilst calling their name.

The child must pretend that the jelly has landed on them and mime getting it off. Then they pretend to pick up a big lump of jelly and throw it at someone else.

Tip: Only do this game if you can be sure the class can calm down again – otherwise it will 'hype them up' too much!

101. The folding puzzle

In this energizer, children are set a challenge to fold a piece of paper as many times as possible.

What you need: sheets of paper of different sizes: A5 up to A2, or as big as possible. The paper can be old or recycled.

What to do:

Start with the smallest piece of paper and ask the children how many times they think they will be able to fold it, folding in half each time? Note their answers.

Then ask a child to fold the paper in half, then half again, until they can't make any more folds.

Have a look at other sizes and ask the children if they will be able to make more folds this time?

They will discover that you can only fold a piece of paper about six or maybe seven times, whatever the size.

102. Invent a game

This energizer encourages children to draw on their own experience to invent games and describe how to play.

What you need: a piece of paper or rough jotter and pencil for each pupil or pair of pupils

What to do:

Children can sit at their desks to do this, working individually or with a neighbour. Ask them to make up a short game that the class could play. This could be a variation on a game the class already plays, or it could be an entirely new game.

Ask them to write in note form the moves and aims of their game, and stress that they need to think out the details.

While they are doing this, go round the class and look for games with potential that you might develop as a class and try out.

Tip: This could be an ongoing exercise to which children return several times. Encourage them to try out their games during wet playtimes, finding out what works, what does not and what needs refining.

103. Hot or cold

In this energizer, one child has to find an object hidden in the room while the rest of the class give hints.

What you need: a small object or soft toy

What to do:

Choose one child to be 'it'.

This child goes out of the room for a few moments while you hide a small object or toy somewhere out of sight but towards the front of the classroom.

The child comes back into the room and is told to look for the object at random. The class members are to call 'warmer', when the child is going towards the object, and 'cooler' when the child is moving away.

If the child is a long way from the object, they can call 'cold' and if they are fairly close they can call 'hot', until the child finds the object.

104. Just stringing along

This energizer is about making visual comparisons – the sort of challenge children love.

What you need: cut two exactly equal lengths of string. Do this again but make the next pair of strings a little longer or shorter than the first pair. Repeat this until you have as many individual strings as there are children in the class.

What to do:

This activity is good for pairing up children in a way they themselves might not usually choose. Mix up the pieces of string or put them in a bowl and ask each child to pick a piece of string. Each then has to seek out the only other child in the class whose string is the same length as their own. Set a time limit for this.

Collect in all the strings at the end, ready to use again for another time, just for fun or to get children ready in pairs for some activity.

105. Slinky

This energizer uses lateral thinking as the teacher uses a spiral toy to get children's attention and fire their imagination.

What you need: a slinky (child's toy – a spiral coil that can motion down a staircase)

What to do:

Stand at the front and, using the slinky, act something that the children have to guess, for instance, holding one end of the slinky to your ear, and the other in front of your face, children have to guess that the slinky is your phone.

Other examples: put the slinky on the desk upright, as if it were a mug with a drink inside, and stir in some sugar; drape the slinky over your shoulders as a scarf; bounce it up and down as a yoyo, or drag one end on the floor and call *'Heel, Rover'* as it is your dog's lead.

106. Topic quiz

This energizer tests memory skills as you ask children questions about their current study topic.

What you need: a pre-prepared question sheet with questions on a current study topic

What to do:

Pick a current topic you are studying (geography, history, science, etc.) Write a list of questions in advance, or pick them from a reference book such as a Dorling Kindersley Eye Witness book on your subject.

Ask the children the questions and they can answer by putting up their hands. You can play this in teams.

It is a useful little tool for assessing how much children have taken in.

Tip: Form the children into teams. Each team has to devise a few questions to ask the others.

107. On the deck

This energizer stimulates children to use their association skills in a game that uses playing cards.

What you need: a pack of playing cards with the picture cards removed

What to do:

With a pack of shuffled playing cards, explain to the children that each suit means a different activity, as follows:

Dig with a Spade	Pretend to dig the garden
Healthy Heart	Jump on the spot while arms wave from side to side
Running Club	Run on the spot
Diamond	An adaptation of the jumping jack, jumping to bring feet together, and bringing hands together up into a diamond point above the head, then jumping with feet and hands.

Start with children standing in a space. A child picks a card at random, looks at it and calls out the activity, and the number – which is how many times they must jump, or move while the child counts down from the number.

108. Autumn leaves

In this energizer, children use their sorting and classification skills with a selection of leaves.

What you need: a bag of mixed autumn leaves which you provide or which children bring in or collect on a walk

What to do:

Ask each child to select, with closed eyes, a leaf from the bag.
You can then put children into random groups by asking them to find others with the same type of leaf.
Alternatively, you can ask them to put themselves in line according to the number of points on their leaves, the size of their leaves or the depth and vividness of autumnal colour.

Tip: Other things to do with leaves:

- show the children an identification chart and ask them to identify their leaves
- have a discussion about how the leaves of bushes and trees change according to season
- draw round the leaves and colour; matching the original as closely as possible
- mime a tree swaying in the breeze or gradually losing its leaves.

109. Charades

This energizer doesn't use words so children have to be inventive and enjoy the thrill of performing for their peers.

What you need: a few slips of paper on which you have written the names of well-known children's films or books

What to do:

Tell the children the rules of charades: one person knows the name of the film or book and stands in front of the class. That person must not talk, but must hold up fingers to say how many words there are in the title.

For instance, *'The Lion, the Witch and the Wardrobe'* would require him to hold up seven fingers. Then, he acts out each word, one at a time, using fingers to show the position of the word in the title: so, he would hold up two fingers before acting out 'lion'.

The class tries to guess each word as it is acted – and when someone has guessed the full title the actor makes a 'thumbs up' sign.

For younger children, keep the titles short and easy.

110. Total recall

While enjoying this energizer, children need to memorize a range of objects on a tray.

What you need: a tray visible to all the children, with a number of objects on it, the more diverse the better: for example, a whistle, blackboard rubber, small toy, hair band, necklace. You also need a piece of paper and pencil for each child.

What to do:

For young children, start with just a few objects, and gradually build on this in future sessions. Let the children see the objects for a limited amount of time, such as one minute. Then cover up the objects. Children must remember what the objects were. Give them three minutes to write down all the objects they can remember.

Tip: Younger children may find this version easier: ask the children to close their eyes while you remove an object, then open their eyes and say which item you removed.

111. Laugh and giggle

This energizer teaches children that laughter is most invigorating.

What you need: lively music and a music player you can stop and start easily

What to do:

Tell the children that laughing is good for them and that this is a good game for cheering everyone up.

Ask them all to stand up.

Their goal is to laugh, giggle and snigger while the music is playing, but when the music stops, they must stop too; they must not even smile! If anyone is caught laughing, giggling or smiling while the music has stopped, they are 'out' and must sit down.

Children who are 'out' may, of course, wish to do whatever they can, silently and without standing, to make the others laugh or giggle at the wrong times!

Tip: Play this game without making any child 'out', simply continuing it until all the children cannot stop laughing and giggling. This is great for morale, for energizing and cheering up the class; but only do this game when you know they can calm down again quickly.

112. Copy cat, copy cat

During this energizer, children work in threes to copy a movement.

What you need: nothing

What to do:

Arrange the children in sets of three. One of the three is to carry out a quick succession of simple movements or activities (such as arranging his or her hair, writing, tidying the table), and the others must copy everything this child does.

Make it more challenging by asking copy-cats to 'mirror' the activities – so, for instance, if the leader does something with the right hand, the copy-cats do it with their left.

113. Football quiz

This energizer is a quiz with the extra motivation of scoring a goal with each correct answer.

What you need: a teacher's whiteboard or blackboard and marker pens or chalk. Some pre-prepared quiz questions to challenge the children. The questions could relate to some work that has recently been completed or needs revising.

What to do:

Divide the class in half, varying the way this is done for different quizzes to make the outcomes less predictable: for example, divide the class front to back, across the middle or diagonally one way or the other.

Tell the children they are in a soccer match and the way to score is to answer a question correctly. Draw two sets of goal posts on the board. Address a quiz question to one half of the class, and if a child provides the correct answer, that side scores. If nobody can answer, the goal is missed and the question is offered to the other side. When a team scores, draw a football in the mouth of the goal.

Tip: To give less-confident children a chance to shine, draw out those who do not normally put their hand up by including questions about hobbies or interests you know they follow.

114. Sumgo!

This energizer is a variation on Bingo but uses sums and practises mental maths.

What you need: a grid with nine boxes on paper or an individual whiteboard for each child. A pencil for each child. A pile of 25 cards for the teacher, with a short sum written on each. The sums must yield an answer for each number from 1 to 25.

What to do:

Ask the children to fill in their grids, choosing any nine numbers between 1 and 25 and writing in any of these in random order, one number in each square.

Shuffle your pile of cards, pick out a card at random and call out the sum. Anyone who has that number on his/her grid draws a line through it.

The first child to cross off all their numbers calls *'SUMGO!'*

You can choose whether to stop there or continue until all the cards have been called.

115. Fun sums

This energizer makes children realize that mental addition can be entertaining and fun.

What you need: some sums of varying difficulty which are suitable for doing mentally

What to do:

Give the children a short sum to do first, as a warm-up. Then make the sums progressively longer.

For instance: *start with one, add on two, plus three, minus two, now take away one, and add on ten, plus two, then add on four, then subtract six.*

116. Möbius band

Your children will be intrigued by this energizer that investigates cutting up a band of paper.

What you need: children need access to a piece of paper (an A4 sheet will do nicely); a pair of scissors; a glue stick or roll of sticky tape; and a coloured pen

What to do:

Ask the child to cut a strip of paper (roughly 4cm wide and 30cm long is a convenient size). Take the two short ends which they are going to join together to form a ring using glue or sticky tape, but before they join them, give the paper one twist, so that the band has a loop in it rather like a figure of eight.

Then stick the ends together.

Now take the felt pen and place it in the middle of the paper.

Tell the child they are going to start drawing a line along the middle of the ring (like a white line up the middle of a road).

Ask them what they think will happen when they get back to where the line started? Ask them to draw the line and find if they were right.

Next, tell them they are going to cut along the line they have drawn. Again, ask them to predict what will happen, and then try it. If they are careful with the cutting, or if they use a wider piece of paper, they could cut it again.

117. Secret leader

In this energizer, children need acute observation to work out who is calling the shots.

What you need: nothing

What to do:

Explain to the children that they are going to follow a leader, but one child will not know who the leader is and will have to guess.

Choose one child to be 'it'. This child goes out of the room for a moment, while you choose another child from those remaining in the room to be the leader.

The leader must lead an activity, such as stretch, lunge, crouch, running on the spot – changing the movements frequently.

If there is not enough space, use hand, arm and head movements, such as tug your ear, turn your head, point to the window. The other children have to follow as closely as possible.

The child who does not know who is leading must try to guess, and the others must do their best to prevent this.

Explain to the children that if they are all facing the leader and looking closely at them, this will give the game away to the person trying to guess.

118. Hot potato

Speed is the exciting element of this energizer as children try not to get caught with the 'hot potato'.

What you need: enough space for a wide circle and a soft object to throw, such as a soft toy or ball

What to do:

Choose one child to be 'it'. This child sits in the middle with eyes closed. Tell the children the object they are going to throw represents a hot potato, and if they hold on to it for too long they will burn their hands.

Give the 'hot potato' to one child, who gets rid of it as quickly as possible by throwing it to any other child, who then throws it to another, and so on. If the potato is dropped or thrown where it cannot be caught, the last child to touch the potato has to fetch it.

After a short time, the person sitting in the middle with closed eyes shouts out *'Hot Potato!'* Whoever is holding the potato is then 'out' and must leave the circle and watch from the side.

The players are gradually eliminated, and the chances of getting caught out increase.

Tip: Speed is the exciting element of this game. Explain to the children that the shorter the time they hold the potato, the less chance they have of being caught out. If throwing and catching are a problem, try the same game with the children passing the potato as quickly as they can.

119. Trust me!

In this energizer, one child leads another whose eyes are closed, thereby developing trust and responsibility.

What you need: some space for children to move around in

What to do:

Explain to the children that they are going to play a game of trust. Each child finds a partner; one child keeps eyes closed and the other leads him or her round the room, taking care not to bump into anyone or anything.

After two minutes, ask them to swap places. If space is limited, try this with half the class at once, as the other half is likely to enjoy watching.

Tip: Get children to discuss the feelings this activity creates. They might be scared of walking into something or someone, or worried that their partner will not do their job properly and will abandon them or lose concentration. Children can then talk about what 'trust' is, and its importance.

120. Times tables stomp

This energizer helps children reinforce their knowledge of tables by marching together and establishing a helpful rhythm.

What you need: nothing

What to do:

The children walk in a crocodile round the room chanting any suitable table together – once three is three, two threes are six, three threes are nine, etc. Make more of a game of this by imposing rules, such as, 'Clap every time the answer is an even number'.